Everything You Need to Know About

TEENS WHO KILL

The easy availability of handguns contributes to the alarming rate of death by gunshot among teens.

• THE NEED TO KNOW LIBRARY •

Everything You Need to Know About

TEENS WHO KILL

Jeffrey A. Margolis

THE ROSEN PUBLISHING GROUP, INC.
NEW YORK

Published in 2000 by The Rosen Publishing Group, Inc.
29 East 21st Street, New York, NY 10010

First Edition

Library of Congress Cataloging-in-Publication Data

Margolis, Jeffrey A.
    Everything you need to know about teens who kill / Jeffrey A. Margolis
       p. cm. — (The need to know library)
    Includes bibliographical references and index.
    Summary: Discusses the phenomenon of teenagers who kill, why these incidents happen, and what society can do to prevent such crimes.
    ISBN 0-8239-2883-7
    1. Juvenile homicide—United States—Juvenile literature. 2. Juvenile delinquency—United States—Juvenile literature. 3. Violent crimes—United States—Juvenile literature. [1. Juvenile homicide. 2. Murder.] I. Title. II. Title: Teens who kill. III. Series.
    HV9067.H6M37 1999
    364.15'23'08350973—dc21
                                    98-45103
                                      CIP
                                      AC

T 42181

Manufactured in the United States of America

Contents

Introduction

The headlines just seemed to keep coming, one right after another. The events they described were similar—and terrifying. That such a tragedy could happen even once was unthinkable. But five times in just seven months?

On the first day of October in 1997, in Pearl, Mississippi, sixteen-year-old Luke Woodham brought a hunting rifle to school. He used it to shoot nine of his schoolmates. Two of them were killed, including his former girlfriend. Earlier that morning, Luke had shot his mother to death.

Two months later, on December 1, 1997, fourteen-year-old Michael Carneal carried five guns and several hundred rounds of ammunition to Heath High School in West Paducah, Kentucky. There he opened fire on a large group of his fellow students who had gathered before school for a prayer meeting. Three students were killed; five more were wounded.

Exactly two weeks afterward, on December 15, 1997, Joseph Todd, also fourteen, brought a .22-caliber rifle to his high school in Stamps, Arkansas. When he arrived, he shot and killed two schoolmates. Todd had been bullied and picked on by other students, but his victims were selected at random.

Four months later, on March 24, 1998, Mitchell Johnson, thirteen, crouched in the brush on a small hill overlooking Westside Middle School in Jonesboro, Arkansas, with his eleven-year-old friend Andrew Golden. The boys should have been in class. Instead, they had stolen Mitchell's stepfather's van and a small arsenal of handguns, rifles, and ammunition. During fifth period, one of them pulled the school's fire alarm. When their teachers and classmates filed out, Andrew and Mitchell opened fire. Four students and one teacher were killed. Nine students and another teacher were wounded.

On May 21, 1998, Kipland Kinkel, fifteen, pulled out several guns and began shooting into the crowd assembled in the cafeteria of Thurston High School in Springfield, Oregon. In about one minute, he had killed two students and wounded twenty-two others. At his home, Kip's mother and father were already dead. He had shot them the night before.

Then, on April 20, 1999, came the deadliest of these rampages. Eric Harris and Dylan Klebold, who were both seniors at Columbine High School in Littleton, Colorado,

Kipland Kinkel was arrested after a shooting spree at his high school. Earlier, he had killed his parents.

shot and killed twelve fellow students and a teacher. They wounded twenty-three others before killing themselves.

These incidents are the most extreme examples of a disturbing trend. Over the last fifteen years or so in the United States, the number of teens who kill has risen tremendously—by almost 200 percent. At the same time, the number of teens who have been killed has risen almost as much. For the first time in American history, teenagers and young adults are the group most likely to kill. Also for the first time, members of this same age group are the most likely members of American society to be the victims of homicide.

Today, more teens die as a result of gunshot wounds than from disease. The U.S. Department of Justice (DOJ) estimates that ten teens are killed every day by handguns. The rise in the number of teens who kill has taken place during a time when the overall rate of murder and serious crime in the United States has declined. (The United States still has the highest homicide rate of any industrialized country, however.)

Why? Although—as you may have suspected—there is not one simple answer, this book will examine many explanations for how and why teens kill. It will also provide some advice and suggestions on how to feel safer in your neighborhood and at school. In addition, you will find a list of resources that can provide information, advice, and help.

A steady diet of violent imagery can desensitize people to real violence.

Chapter 1

Who Kills?

*J*esse was frightened. He was beginning to understand why grown-ups got so upset sometimes when they watched the news or read the newspaper. Stories about war and natural disasters had always seemed as if they were happening somewhere else, very far away. But tonight, the first story on the news sounded like something that could happen to him or his friends.

The TV reporter said that Michael Bennett was only fourteen. His mother said, "He's so nice, he's so quiet, he's as good as gold." The principal at Michael's school said that Michael was "one of the school's brightest stars." His teacher said, "He was a vital part of the classroom, extremely pleasant, a nice kid with a good sense of humor, and a good student. He was a kid worried about his grades, so polite . . . I really expected a lot from him." One of his friends said, "He was just cool, just made friends with everyone. Everyone knew Michael Bennett."

Michael had gone out that night to play basketball at a school gym in his neighborhood in Brooklyn, New York. Michael was on a team in a local community league. He idolized Michael Jordan, but he wanted to be a jet pilot when he grew up. On this night, Michael scored thirty-five of his team's fifty-one points. But near the end of the game, which Michael's team won, there was an argument about the score.

Afterward, as Michael was walking home with a friend, a group of kids from the other team jumped them. Michael and his friend tried to run. His friend ran to a gas station, where the gang caught him and hit him in the head with a baseball bat. Michael didn't even make it that far. He was stabbed twice on the street and died fifteen minutes later.

For Jesse, the story was terrifying. They showed a picture of Michael on the news, and he looked a lot like Jesse. He was the same age, too, and just about the same size. Jesse also loved to play basketball, and he liked school, and he had a whole lot of exciting plans for the future. Usually the news didn't seem to have much to do with him or his friends, but this seemed very real. Brooklyn was far away from where Jesse lived, but somehow this event seemed as if it had happened very close to home.

Who Are the Teens that Kill?

Every day in the United States, on average, twenty-two

Arguments and rage often lead to violence.

youths are the victims of homicide. Their killers are most likely to be other youths. Most of these violent acts are committed on weekdays between two in the afternoon and six in the evening. These are after-school hours, when many teens are unsupervised and do not have constructive ways to spend their time.

Until recently, school was regarded as a place safe from such violence. But as the violent acts described in the Introduction show, this is no longer the case. Some schools in New York City and other urban areas require students to pass through metal detectors before they are admitted to school. In the 1998 school year, more than 6,000 students were expelled for carrying guns to school. That same year, there were fifteen deaths and fifty-five injuries as a result of shootings in schools.

Although schools are not as safe as they once were, most homicides that involve teens still take place away from school grounds. They are also unlikely to involve the kinds of crimes that Luke Woodham, Michael Carneal, Joseph Todd, Andrew Golden, Mitchell Johnson, Kipland Kinkel, Eric Harris, and Dylan Klebold committed. Those boys are very extreme examples of teens who kill. What these events have in common is that each boy shot at a large group, selecting his victims mostly at random.

A typical teen homicide is more like the tragedy that happened to Michael Bennett. Teens who kill are much more likely to kill one victim at a time than attempt to murder or injure a large group all at once. The victim is likely to be known to them in some way. If not, the victim is likely to have been chosen after some kind of hostile encounter, such as an argument over a basketball game. Indeed, arguments or disputes are the most common reason for their actions given by teens who kill.

The Bennett case is also typical because five boys instead of just one were eventually arrested for the murder. The most typical teen homicide involves a group that acts as the aggressor against a single individual. The most common type of such group violence is gang activity. According to some government studies, in three out of four murders committed against young people, the killer is likely to be a gang member. The rate of murder resulting from teen gang violence has increased sevenfold since 1976.

Gang activity perpetuates violence against and among young people.

The Bennett case is also typical because the teen who kills is almost always a boy, and the typical victim is a boy. However, guns, not knives, are the most common weapon, and teens who are killed are more likely to have been shot than stabbed. In more than half of all homicides involving teens, a gun is used.

A Big-City Problem?

Many people think of gun use and homicide by teens as an urban problem, the kind of things that happen to kids like Michael Bennett, who live in places like New York City, Los Angeles, or Washington, DC. In terms of sheer numbers, this is true. In recent years, five American cities—Los Angeles, New York, Chicago,

Detroit, and Houston—have accounted for about 25 percent of juvenile homicides. Big cities, many people think, have special problems that do not seem as prevalent in smaller towns. Such problems include poverty, drug abuse, domestic violence, gang activity, poor schools, and racial and ethnic tensions.

It is true that big cities do have these kinds of problems, and it is also true that these problems can be among the factors that lead teens to kill. What is not true is that these problems do not exist outside of big cities. Teen homicide is not just an inner-city problem.

Many people are surprised to learn that in the United States, the murder rate is highest in the parts of the country that are the least urban—the South and the West. (The murder rate is not simply the total number of homicides committed, but rather the frequency of homicide within a given population.)

The same is true of teen homicides. The school shootings you have read about all took place in the South and the West. Throughout history, the South has always been the most rural area of the United States. It has also always had the highest rate of violent crime and murder. Today, the states with the highest rates of homicide— and teen homicide—are Arkansas, Louisiana, Texas, and Oklahoma. The next highest are Alabama, Mississippi, Kentucky, and Tennessee.

Perhaps one explanation for this is that the South has always had an extremely high rate of gun ownership. Although only 35 percent of households in the United

States own a gun, 74 percent of gun owners own two or more firearms. And the rate of gun ownership is much higher in the South than in the other regions of the United States. According to a recent study performed by the National Institute of Justice (NIJ), which is a branch of the U.S. Department of Justice, "middle-aged, college educated people in small rural towns are the most likely to own guns."

One result is that no one in Jonesboro, Arkansas, for example, thought it was unusual that thirteen-year-old Mitchell Johnson proved to be an excellent shot. "Everyone at Westside [Middle School] knows how to shoot a gun," a seventh-grader there explained.

One of the most likely indicators of who will eventually own a gun is whether an individual's parents own firearms. In the NIJ study, 80 percent of gun owners reported that their parents had owned guns. In the four school shootings that took place in the South, the killers all used guns that belonged to their parents. The semi-automatic rifle that Kipland Kinkel turned on his schoolmates in Springfield, Oregon, had been given to him by his father as a gift.

Chapter 2

Why Do Teens Kill?

*T*he funeral was the saddest thing that Angelina had ever experienced. She hadn't known the boy that well; he was only in a couple of her classes. But she knew his name, and he always said hello to her in the hall, and he didn't seem to be a troublemaker. He was too young to be dead; she knew that much. At the funeral, she couldn't believe the pain that was on his mother's face. "Kids aren't supposed to die," Angelina thought. "And they are not supposed to kill each other either. How could someone do something like that? Why *would* someone do something like that?"

If there is anything that seems as unnatural as the death of a child, it might be a child who kills. And teens, after all, are still children, even as they approach adulthood and start to try out adult behavior and roles.

So why would a child kill? And why, in recent years, have teens begun to kill so much more frequently?

Young Men

If teens kill more often than any other age group, does that mean that there is something about being a teenager today that makes one more likely to kill? Not necessarily. Traditionally, in any society, young men are the group most likely to commit violent crime.

In the United States today that remains true. The person most likely to be involved in a homicide, either as the killer or the victim, is a male between the ages of eighteen and twenty-four. The next most likely is a boy between the ages of fourteen and seventeen. Teenage girls very rarely kill. When they do, they rarely kill strangers. Most often, they kill an abusive family member.

There are several reasons why this might be true in any society. Differences in hormones and the way boys are raised are two possible explanations given for why males are more prone to violence than females. Young men, in particular, have greater difficulty in controlling the emotions that lead to violent acts. Usually, teens who kill do not plan to commit murder. Most often the killing is an act of anger or rage or an emotional response to an unplanned situation that gets out of control. In many societies, young men are the group most likely to find themselves outside of the family and work settings that provide stability and emotional support.

These emotions, and the skills and resources needed

to handle them, do seem to be related to youth. After young adulthood, the rates of violent crime, including homicide, move sharply downward as one gets older.

Once again, many explanations are given for why this might be true. Perhaps as people get older they simply find more constructive ways to deal with their emotions. Maybe they grow more skilled at avoiding the kinds of confrontation that lead to violence. Maybe they also learn or find ways to resolve such confrontations nonviolently. Some experts believe that in men the propensity toward violence simply "burns itself out" as they become older.

Inherited or Learned?

None of these explanations completely explain why some young men make it through their youth without any trouble while others get caught up in committing violent acts and even murder. Some experts believe that violence has a biological basis. These scientists argue that a tendency toward violent behavior is passed on from adult to child in the genes. This does not mean that someone who inherits such a tendency is "fated" to commit murder. Instead, experts believe that such a person is more likely to react violently in certain situations than another person of the same age.

Some studies have shown that a large percentage of teens who kill suffer from brain damage. As a rule, teens who kill show poor verbal skills and do poorly on intelligence tests. The young man most recently executed in this country for killing while he was a teen was Dwight Allen Wright, who was put to death on October 14, 1998, in

Growing up in a violent family may make a person more likely to behave violently.

Virginia. He had suffered brain damage as a child and had been diagnosed as borderline retarded. Many teens who kill also suffer from mental illness.

One of the few scientific studies conducted on this subject was published in the *American Journal of Psychiatry* about ten years ago. The study examined fourteen young men who were on death row for murders they had committed while they were teens. Every one of them showed signs of brain damage or learning difficulties. All of them had suffered severe head injuries while they were children. All of them had severe psychiatric difficulties. Most had never been treated by a psychiatrist or received any kind of help or counseling for their problems.

But many other scientists believe that violence is a

learned behavior. They think that teens who commit homicide and other violent acts have most likely been taught or have learned to respond with violence to confrontations and other stressful situations. These scientists believe that teens who grow up in a violent environment are more likely to behave violently. In the *American Journal of Psychiatry* study, for example, all but two of the young men examined had suffered extreme physical and sexual abuse. In most of those cases, the abuse was committed by a family member.

Is Society to Blame?

Although young men are the group most likely to commit violent crime in any society, the rate at which teens kill in the United States is much higher than in similar nations. For example, in the United States in 1995, 5,000 children under the age of nineteen died from gunshot wounds. The majority of those who did the killing were also teenagers.

That same year, only 153 people under the age of nineteen were killed by gunshot in Canada. Only 109 died the same way in France. Only nineteen were murdered with guns in the United Kingdom. In Japan in 1995, no teenagers were killed with guns. Even when one takes into account variations in population between the United States and these nations, the differences are startling. According to the Violence Policy Center, a study group, "twelve times more children are killed by guns in America than in the other twenty-five industrialized countries combined."

So is U.S. society more violent than those of other

industrialized nations? In some ways, it is—but why is that? A number of different explanations have been given. But one reason that clearly stands out above all others is the sheer number of guns that are available in this country.

Many people who have analyzed this issue conclude that is almost impossible to say why an individual teen resorts to pulling the trigger of a gun in a particular situation. What they *are* sure about is that the situation would certainly have ended differently if the teen did not have a gun. The rate of homicide committed by teenagers with guns rose 249 percent between 1985 and 1995. The obvious conclusion is that having a gun makes it easier to kill.

The Right to Bear Arms

Of the industrialized nations, the United States is by far the most heavily armed. We are not talking here about the size of a country's armed forces but about the number of guns owned by a nation's private citizens. By this standard, the United States is far and away the world's leader.

There are an estimated 200 million privately owned firearms in the United States. These include handguns and pistols; so-called long guns, such as rifles and shotguns; and a rapidly increasing number of assault weapons, such as the automatic and semiautomatic rifles used by the military. The number 200 million represents almost one gun for every American citizen. Almost 70 percent of the people who own a handgun also own a rifle or shotgun.

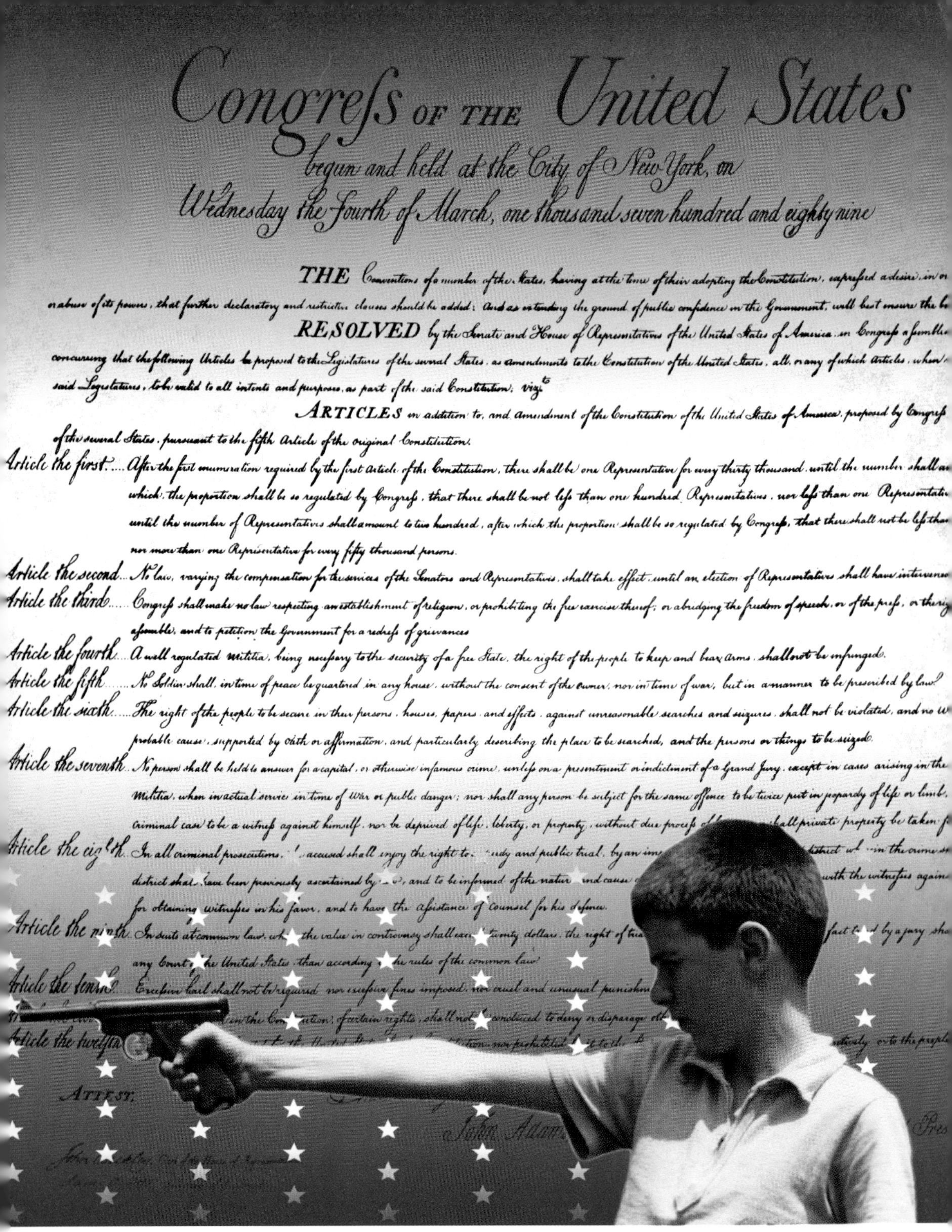

The Second Amendment does not extend to children.

Most gun owners give "protection against crime" as their reason for owning a firearm. For adults, the right to bear arms is guaranteed by the Second Amendment of the U.S. Constitution. This right has been consistently interpreted by courts as giving private citizens the right to own firearms with some limitations.

Perhaps because the United States is a relatively young nation that is very proud of its frontier and pioneer past, gun ownership is deeply rooted in American culture. Many gun owners react strongly to any attempt to regulate gun ownership. They regard such efforts as an infringement upon their constitutional rights and their ability to protect themselves.

Though gun owners may feel that having a gun makes them more secure in their homes, no one can be certain that gun ownership actually prevents crime. What is clear is that the number of crimes committed with guns in the United States is much, much higher than in comparable countries.

The sheer number of guns in the United States makes it inevitable that a large number of guns will wind up in the hands of those who should not have them—criminals and young people. The manufacture and sale of handguns is big business. A handgun is manufactured every ten seconds in the United States. This easy availability helps to keep the cost of guns relatively low. On the street, high-powered firearms often sell for $100 or less. In some places it is even possible to rent a gun.

And the weapons available are increasingly powerful.

Guns are cheap and plentiful in the United States.

In recent years an especially alarming trend has been the increased availability of assault weapons. These are rifles that fire a large number of shots very rapidly with just a single squeeze of the trigger. The Uzi submachine gun, which is made in Israel, and the Kalashnikov or AK-47, which is made in Russia, are particularly popular weapons of this kind. Among the school shooters, for example, Kip Kinkel, as well as Eric Harris and Dylan Klebold, used semiautomatic or assault-type weapons.

As more criminals armed themselves with such weapons, police departments across the country complained that they were being "outgunned." Many then sought to increase their own firepower. For example, in September 1997, police officers in Los Angeles began to be equipped with M-16 assault rifles. The M-16s were surplus weapons originally manufactured for use by the U.S. Army.

Easier access to higher-caliber and faster-firing weapons means a greater chance that a gunshot wound will result in the death of the victim. Such weapons also tend to be less accurate, especially in the hands of inexperienced users. This increases the likelihood that bystanders to a shooting will also be hit.

Safe or Sorry?

One consequence of the proliferation of guns in the United States is that more people feel the need to own guns in order to protect themselves against others with firearms. A sense of safety is a fragile thing, and every new story of a crime committed with a gun makes others feel that they need to protect themselves in the same way.

Just as most gun owners report that they keep weapons in the home for protection, an increasing number of teenagers say that they carry guns for the same reason. A 1995 survey showed that one out of twelve students reported carrying a gun for protection.

Such fears may be understandable, but teens need to be very, very careful when making that decision. In most states, juveniles are not legally allowed to own or carry firearms. And a confrontation or argument cannot be settled at the point of a gun if neither party to the disagreement has one.

Chapter 3

Motives

You have now read about some of the more general explanations for the rise in the number of teens who kill. But what goes on in the mind of a teen who kills? What makes one teen kill when another in a similar situation does not?

Emotionally, adolescence can be a stormy time. Teens are growing into adulthood both physically and psychologically. This growth takes place rapidly and causes many changes, some of which can be very stressful to deal with. It is no surprise then that issues of identity, self-worth, and belonging become very important. Teens may also experiment with behaviors that place them in high-risk situations. All of these factors need to be considered when one thinks about why a teen might kill.

Risky Business

According to the U.S. Department of Justice (DOJ), the two most common circumstances in which homicides are committed are arguments and other criminal behavior. The DOJ defines arguments as "brawls due to the influence of narcotics or alcohol, disagreements about money or property and other disputes." By criminal behavior, the government means a situation in which a person sets out to commit a crime other than murder. In the course of committing that crime, through various circumstances, a homicide takes place.

What both of these circumstances have in common is that the original intent of the killer was not to kill. But by engaging in risky or criminal behavior, the chance of a teen's being involved in a homicide—either as the victim or the perpetrator—greatly increases. There are an enormous number of reasons why teens may become involved in criminal behavior or find themselves in the kind of situation where a violent argument takes place. The most common reason is the use of alcohol or other drugs.

Obviously, most teens who experiment with alcohol or drugs do not commit any crimes, let alone murder. But an enormously high percentage of teens who are arrested for crimes—up to 90 percent—have a history of alcohol or drug use. One study indicates that 73 percent of teens who kill were intoxicated on alcohol or drugs at the time.

Violence and drugs often go hand in hand.

Just as drug use impairs judgment and weakens emotional control, causing teens to engage in risky behavior in the first place, it also leads to making the kind of poor decisions that create an even worse situation. A robbery turns into a shooting; an argument becomes violent. And just using alcohol or drugs is more likely to put you in a place where trouble can happen.

Teens who get involved in dealing drugs are also much more likely to kill. Experts link the rise in the use of guns by teens with the arrival of crack cocaine in many neighborhoods in the mid-1980s. As teen drug dealers began to use guns to defend their share of the drug business, an increasing number of other teens felt the need to carry guns for protection.

Drug and alcohol use plays one more role in teen homicides. Statistics show that the use of drugs or alcohol increases the likelihood that you will be the victim of a violent crime, especially homicide.

Gangs: A Need to Belong

For teens in particular, gang activity is an especially frequent factor that leads to teen homicide. Gangs have a long history in this country, dating back to the early eighteenth century in some American cities. Today, although many people continue to think of them as a big-city problem, gangs can be found in just about every state. According to some reports, there may be more than 3,800 gangs in this country with a total membership of more than 200,000 people.

Generally, gangs tend to be all-male organizations, but there are all-female gangs as well. The most important thing a gang offers its members is group identity, a sense of solidarity, and belonging. Gangs create this identity through their name, their "colors" or logo, tattoos, some distinctive style of dress, hand signals, and their own code of honor.

The code of honor almost always involves an initiation rite. The purpose of the initiation is to bind the new member permanently to the gang, which is often seen as a new family. By undergoing the initiation, the new member proves himself worthy of joining the group.

Symbolically, the new member does this by showing that he or she is willing to leave behind the values of the old group and society in general and embrace the new values of the gang. Frequently, this is accomplished through a criminal act, such as a robbery or assault, or by the new member's allowing himself or herself to be the victim of violence. This last method often takes the form of a group beating by the gang, an ordeal called "jumping in." By taking part in such rituals, the new member proves his willingness to uphold the gang's highest value—loyalty to the gang. Many gangs consider membership to be a lifetime commitment.

Another Family

Gangs appeal to youths who are unable to find a sense of belonging anywhere else. Most people find this sense of belonging within their family. It is therefore no surprise that many gang members have a troubled family history and that they regard their gang as a surrogate or substitute family. The gang gives members a sense of identity and belonging that is missing at home. Such individuals usually have a very poor sense of who they are. They are much more comfortable identifying themselves as a member of a group than as an individual.

Many gangs draw on the shared ethnic identity of members as a reason for their solidarity. Their members are often all people of a specific ethnic, racial, or minority group. Many times, the members of such groups are economically or socially disadvantaged and feel discriminated against. Membership in a gang allows individuals to feel a sense of status and importance that they do not otherwise feel in the larger community.

Some gangs exist essentially as criminal enterprises. Sales of guns and weapons are a common gang activity. Violence and homicide quite often follow. Gangs have used guns regularly since the 1970s, mainly to protect their turf in the drug business. Gang members are especially interested in semiautomatic weapons such as Uzis and AK-47s. Until recent changes were made in juvenile-crime laws, gangs actively recruited younger and younger members. Such "shorties" were used as drug couriers and in other crimes because if caught they were too young to be sentenced to jail.

Because group identity is so important to gangs, rivalries with similar groups take on exaggerated importance that inevitably leads to violence. This rivalry results in gang warfare over turf, business opportunities, and "respect." The targets of such violence are picked more or less at random; in such cases, the sole reason for a victim to be targeted is membership in a rival group. This is often the case in so-called drive-by shootings, which over the past fifteen years have become an increasingly common way that teens kill.

The hostility in Los Angeles between the two gangs known as the Crips and the Bloods is perhaps the best known of these rivalries. The murders of enormously popular rap stars Tupac Shakur and Biggie Smalls are believed by some to have been related to disagreements between gangs.

The killing of Tupac Shakur may have been linked to gang violence.

"Don't Dis Me"

An enormous number of the arguments and confrontations that lead teens to kill revolve around the issue of respect. For teens who are struggling with questions of identity and self-worth, acceptance and respect from others, especially their peers, are extremely important. For such teens, behavior that suggests that they are being disrespected, or "dissed," can provoke an extreme reaction. Years ago the disputes that arose from such situations might have been settled with fists. Today, sadly, they are much more likely to be settled with guns.

Respect is also at the heart of the increasing number of murders that involve one teen's killing another over an item of clothing or jewelry. In many cases teens have killed in order to obtain an expensive pair of basketball sneakers, gold jewelry, or a leather jacket. For many teens, these items are status symbols. Unsure of their own self-worth, they believe that owning such things will make them more important and earn the respect of others. This can be especially true of teens who have grown up in poverty.

Sometimes the teens who kill are what are called "wannabes." They feel powerless in their own life and want to belong to a group that will allow them to feel more important and powerful. One way they do this is by imitating the "gangbangers" they read about in the papers, see depicted in movies or television, or hear celebrated in some rap music.

The ultimate way they choose to do so is by committing the ultimate bad act—killing someone. According to his classmates, Mitchell Johnson—the teen who shot his schoolmates in Jonesboro, Arkansas—said that "he'd give anything to be in a gang. He'd kill anyone to be in a gang." He even started wearing red, the color of the Bloods, and telling his friends that he was a member of that gang.

Dying for Love

For many teens, there is no more important—and stressful—issue than romantic relationships. Trouble in these relationships is often among the factors that motivate teens to kill. A frequent cause of violence is jealousy over a boyfriend or girlfriend. Respect is also a factor here. The boys who killed Michael Bennett in Brooklyn believed he had dissed one of their girlfriends, who was

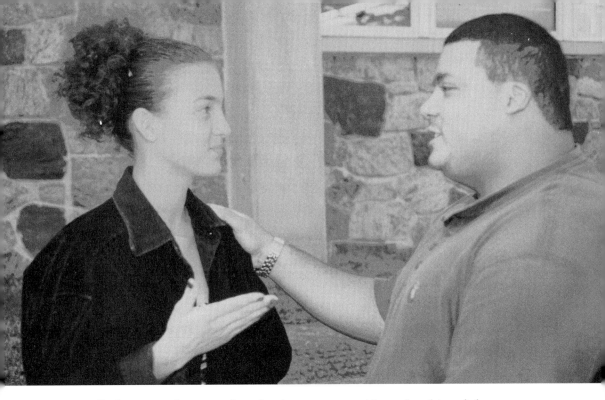

Jealousy and romantic rejection can sometimes lead to violence.

acting as the scorekeeper for the basketball game at which the dispute arose.

Another possible cause of violence is romantic rejection. Teens with a poor sense of their own self-worth overreact—sometimes violently—to such rejection. Luke Woodham, Michael Carneal, and Mitchell Johnson had all been rejected by girls not long before the shootings. Often, such teens first threaten suicide before deciding to kill someone else. Again, the teens who kill in these circumstances are almost invariably boys.

Rejection in general is an extremely common factor in violent crime. Many teens who kill have been bullied or picked on in school or on the streets. Many have trouble making friends and maintaining relationships, often because they have low verbal skills or are otherwise developmentally challenged.

Family troubles are also a common factor that leads teens to kill. One of the most frequent problems among teens who kill is physical or sexual abuse by a parent or adult caretaker. Some studies have shown that 10 percent of youths who commit homicide kill a parent or a parent's sexual partner. And the single most common experience among teens who kill is domestic violence.

Teens who have been abused are also much more likely to act out violently against someone outside of the family. At her brother's funeral, Michael Bennett's younger sister put it this way: "I don't know why they killed him. Maybe because he had a family that loved him, and they didn't have a family that loved them."

Bias Crimes

Issues of self-respect, identity, and sexuality are all involved in so-called bias crimes, where violence is directed toward an individual who is perceived by others as being different. That difference may be based on racial or ethnic identity, language, appearance, or sexual orientation.

For example, in 1989, teenager Yusuf Hawkins was shot and killed by a group of teens in Bensonhurst, Brooklyn. Yusuf was black; his killers were white. He had gone to Bensonhurst, a predominantly white community, to check out a used car he was interested in buying. Yusuf's killers attacked him because he did not "belong" in "their" neighborhood.

Similarly, in 1993, Brandon Teena was murdered by two schoolmates in Humboldt, Nebraska. Brandon, a newcomer to Humboldt, had become very popular, especially with the girls at school. But Brandon was also hiding a secret. Although Brandon looked, dressed, acted, and was accepted as a boy, "he" was really a girl. When Brandon's secret was revealed, she became an outcast—and ultimately a target of rape and murder by two boys who were enraged by the deception.

Brandon Teena's choice to live as a boy was a threat to the sexual or gender identity—the sense of what it means to be a man or a woman—of her killers. Likewise, in the case of Yusuf Hawkins, Yusuf's racial identity was seen as a threat to the identity of members of another group. In these incidents, the teens who killed were unsure of their own self-worth and looked for status through some larger group—where all members are white, for example, or straight. Anyone outside of the group is seen as a potential target of prejudice or even violence resulting from those biases.

Poverty

The most common factor in all the issues that lead teens to kill is poverty. Being poor puts one at much greater risk of being affected by alcohol and drug use, family troubles, educational difficulties, mental and emotional illness, gang activity, and criminal behavior as either a participant or witness. A typical teen killer comes from a family with a single parent at home, where one or both parents have a history of drug abuse, mental illness, or criminal behavior and are neglectful or abusive. All of these problems are more common among people who are poor.

Issues of identity and respect often become even more important to teens who live in poverty. And despite its wealth, the United States has an enormous number of children—an estimated 17 million—who are poor. This is a much higher percentage than similar wealthy nations, such as Japan, France, England, or Germany.

When money becomes so important in determining social status, as is true in the United States, poverty can be enormously damaging to one's sense of self-worth. Related issues, such as racial discrimination, can have similar effects. Because the United States is such a tremendously wealthy society that also takes great pride in the idea of equality, poor people can be made to feel that poverty is their own fault. Likewise, some of the more well-off members of society believe that poverty is the result of a person's moral failing or a character flaw.

Media Violence

There is little doubt that a child who witnesses or directly experiences acts of violence while growing up is more likely to commit an act of violence. An increasing number of concerned adults and teens are asking whether exposure to violence in the media can have the same effect.

It has been estimated that by the time a typical child in the United States reaches the age of eighteen, he or she will have "witnessed" as many as 8,000 murders—

Various factors make some teens more likely to commit violence than others.

and 200,000 other violent acts—on television, at the movies, in music videos and video games, and in books, magazines, newspapers, and music lyrics.

According to a study by the American Psychological Association, more than half of the shows on television regularly depict acts of violence—usually a shooting, a fight, or a beating. In many of these shows, the hero uses an act of violence to solve his or her problems.

Although some experts disagree, many doctors, scientists, and educators believe that media violence desensitizes vulnerable youths to the point where they are more likely to commit violent acts in real life. After they kill, these teens often appear stunned or astounded, as if they cannot understand the consequences of their action or even believe that it is real. It is as if repeated exposure to violence has left them numb to its consequences in real life. Even before he killed, Kipland Kinkel described himself as overstimulated by "role-playing games, heavy metal music, violent cartoons/TV, sugared cereal."

Chapter 4

Consequences

You do not have to be a killer, a victim, or a witness to suffer from the acts of teens who kill. Perhaps a fellow student has been killed by another teen. Maybe you know of a family that has been devastated by such a tragedy. Maybe you do not feel as safe at school or elsewhere, or maybe there are places you would like to go and things you would like to do that your parents won't allow because they worry about your safety. Perhaps you don't like the fact that some adults believe that teenagers are not just irresponsible but also dangerous. Or maybe you just think it is sad that so many youths in this society are driven to commit such desperate acts.

One thing is certain—American citizens are frightened by the rise in the numbers of teens who kill. More than anything, people are fed up but don't quite know what to do about the problem.

Crime and Punishment

One response of American society has been to change the way in which teens who commit violent crimes are treated by the legal system. For almost a century, the U.S. legal system considered crimes committed by minors—those under the age of eighteen—under different rules than those committed by adults.

For juveniles, the emphasis was on their age rather than the crime committed. Because minors were not yet adults, the focus was on rehabilitation rather than punishment for their criminal acts. Minors were tried for their crimes in special juvenile courts, not the regular criminal courts where adults were tried.

When handing out sentences, judges were supposed to consider the best interests of the child as well as the best interests of society. That usually meant trying to find a sentence that offered the juvenile criminal some kind of program or treatment from which he or she could learn a more productive way to behave. The belief was that because of their youth, even teens who had committed violent crimes deserved a chance to reform themselves. This approach was extended even to teens who killed.

But over the last fifteen years or so, the attitude has been changing. As the overall rate of violent teen crime has increased, so has society's demand that violent teens—especially teens who kill—be tried and punished as adults. The reasoning seems to be that those who are old enough to commit such violent acts are also old enough to be treated as adults in the legal system.

Ultimate Crime, Ultimate Penalty

At the same time, society's attitude toward crime in general has become harsher. Frustrated by rising crime rates, a majority of Americans has come to favor more severe punishment of criminals.

As with teens, the emphasis has shifted away from rehabilitation to punishment. Americans have become less and less interested in trying to figure out why criminals behave as they do. Instead, the focus has shifted to longer prison sentences. This new attitude might be described as "You did the crime, now do the time."

The result has been new laws that create much harsher prison sentences and that take away much of a judge's discretion to consider the specific circumstances surrounding a particular criminal's actions. These statutes are sometimes referred to as "mandatory minimum" or "three strikes and you're out" laws. For those who kill, the changes have also meant the return of capital punishment, also known as the death penalty.

From 1966 to 1977 in the United States, no criminals were executed for their crimes. But since 1977, thirty-eight states have passed death penalty laws. Twenty-nine of those states have carried out executions since 1977, and more than 500 people have been put to death since then. All but a handful were adult men.

These changes have affected teenage criminals, including teens who kill, in much the same way. Today, all fifty states allow teenagers to be tried as adults, outside of juvenile court, for criminal acts. Twenty-six of those states allow children *of any age* to be tried as adults. In eighteen others, teens above the age of fourteen can be tried as adults. In Louisiana, teens older than fifteen can be tried as adults. In the remaining five states, the minimum age ranges from seven to thirteen.

These new laws also mean that teens who kill may also pay the ultimate price for their crimes—execution. Thirty-eight states now have a death penalty for teens convicted of certain kinds of murder. Currently seventy-three people, all men, are on death row in the United States for murders they committed as teens. Texas and Florida have more individuals on death row for crimes committed while they were teens than all the other states combined. Since 1977, twelve young men in six states have been executed for crimes committed while they were teens.

The United States' use of the death penalty makes it unusual among nations. For example, no European nation currently uses capital punishment. Since 1990, only five other countries have legally executed teens who kill—Iran, Pakistan, Yemen, Saudi Arabia, and Nigeria. Of the nations who use the death penalty, the United States has executed the most young men for homicides committed while teens. The United States also has the most juveniles on death row of any nation.

Another View

Not all Americans agree that harsher punishments are the best way to stop rising crime. Several organizations are working to get state and federal governments to change the laws concerning the execution of teens who kill. The "Stop Killing Kids" program, for example, maintains that the failure of families and schools to properly educate young people has led to the increase in juvenile homicide. Stop Killing Kids looks for ways to teach young people coping skills, so that they do not resort to violent behavior as a way to solve their problems.

Professor Ira Schwartz of the University of Michigan, who has studied the causes of teen violence, agrees with this reasoning. He says that "until we realize we need every child in this country to be healthy, well-fed, and educated, we're heading in the wrong direction."

Dealing with Death

When teens kill, the focus is usually on the killer and victim. Often forgotten are those who are left behind to deal with the consequences of the violent act—friends and family members in particular.

As a result of the rise in the number of teens who kill other teens, more and more young people, at an earlier age, must cope with the death of a friend or relative as a result of violence. In some cities, young people tell of going to more funerals in a year than school dances.

Dealing with grief over the death of a loved one is an extremely difficult process to go through. Studies

Losing friends or family members to violence is
deeply disturbing.

have shown that grief can be even more complicated
for teens who lose close friends to violence or who have
directly witnessed a homicide. Aside from the normal
feelings that result—anger, rage, shock, denial, and
sadness—there is a feeling of helplessness. Inability
to work through these feelings can lead to problems
later on, including depression and the acting out of
angry impulses.

It is not uncommon for young people who have never
had to deal with these feelings before to seem lost. The
sudden violent death of another teen is deeply disturbing. For many young people, such a tragedy forces
them to realize consciously—perhaps for the first
time—that they are not in complete control of their

lives and that merely being at the wrong place at the wrong time can be deadly.

Other teens find that they have a difficult time concentrating in school after a violent experience. Still others have dreams and nightmares about the incident. Some develop physical symptoms. Young people in these situations need time to mourn and freedom to express the anger and sadness that they feel.

Five Stages

Psychologists have identified five separate stages of grief that young people go through when someone close to them dies. They are:

- Shock—The survivor has a hard time believing what has happened. He or she may feel "nothing" or "numb" about the incident.
- Denial—The survivor attempts to deny the importance of what has happened, insisting that everything is all right or that the loss is not really affecting him or her.
- Sadness—Sorrow about the magnitude of the loss sets in as the survivor begins to fully realize and understand what has happened.
- Anger—The survivor displays rage and frustration about the loss, although often in circumstances that seem unrelated to the killing. This anger may be displayed toward people close to the survivor, or be self-directed in the form of guilt or depression.

• Anxiety—The survivor experiences a new sense of insecurity about aspects of his or her life and may seek to avoid experiences that remind him or her of the loss.

There is no set time frame for going through these stages. Grieving is a process that has its own schedule. It can continue for several weeks to several months and even for several years, and it cannot be rushed or hurried.

Talk It Out

It is extremely important for young people in this situation to express their feelings. This can be difficult to do. After a traumatic event, many young people shut down and refuse to talk about their deep feelings, either because it is too painful or because they feel it is tougher or braver to keep them inside.

The hardest thing to do is to find someone you trust enough to talk to about the situation. You can start with a friend, but often more experienced help is necessary. Find an adult you can trust. Try a teacher, counselor, member of the clergy, doctor, coach, or relative. Someone at your school should be able to help you or guide you to someone who can. After the March 1998 shootings at the Westside Middle School in Jonesboro, Arkansas, for example, more than eighty counselors and psychologists were brought to the school to help students and their families.

Above all, young people should not be afraid to grieve. It is a necessary part of the healing process.

Chapter 5

What You Can Do

Just as there is no absolute way to know which teens will kill or why they kill, there is no single way to ensure that teens will not ever kill. Still, there are things that can be done to make your world a safer place. By doing so, you can increase your own sense of safety and security and make others feel safer as well. And in a safer world, it is hoped that teens will be less likely to kill.

Fight or Flight

Anger is the most basic of the emotions that lead teens to kill. Anger can have many different causes. But no matter what the cause, dealing with anger is a skill that can be learned and improved upon.

Everyone gets angry at one time or another. Sometimes the cause of anger is immediately apparent, like being turned down for a date, threatened, or disciplined. Anger can also be a more constant feeling, brought about by bigger or long-term problems, such as the death of a loved one or family issues.

The human body reacts to anger in several ways. The blood pressure rises and the heart beats faster; muscles may tense. Anger also releases chemicals into the bloodstream that help us prepare for "fight" or "flight."

Fight or flight are the most basic responses to anger and to fear, which is closely related to anger. Sometimes, either response is useful. If someone tries to attack you on the street, for example, defending yourself or running away can be a useful reaction.

But in most everyday situations, neither response is particularly useful. And uncontrolled anger, obviously, can result in violence. Boys and men, especially, have a much harder time controlling anger than do girls and women.

The process of dealing with feelings of anger, fear, or distress is sometimes referred to as impulse control. Most of the time, teens who kill do not plan to do so. Instead, they act out of impulse. Teens who are angry sometimes do not even know exactly what triggers their angry reaction. Very often, teens who kill are unable to give any real reason afterward for their action. The only explanation they can provide is something along the lines of "I just snapped" or "I just did it."

Controlling Anger

Although anger must be controlled, it is also unhealthy to allow it to build up inside of you. After all, anger is

Exercise is a healthy and safe way to release pent-up anger.

a quite natural—and unavoidable—response to certain events. But there are ways to let it out without injuring other people or property.

First, you must learn to identify what causes your anger. Then think about steps you can take to release it constructively. Because the body responds to anger physically, there are physical ways to rid yourself of anger. They include:

- Physical activity—Try exercise or some other activity that takes your mind off the immediate situation.
- Time-out—Simply remove yourself from the situation. Walk away and try to relax. Discuss your concerns with a friend. It is always a good idea to

think before responding to any situation, let alone
one that makes you mad.
• Breathing exercises and relaxation techniques—A
therapist or even a qualified exercise instructor can
teach you to breathe and move in a way that allows
your body to release anger.

At times, everyone needs to reach out to someone else
for help in dealing with anger. This might be as simple
as talking things out with a friend, but you may also
need to talk with a parent, teacher, counselor, doctor, or
therapist. All people, but especially boys, need to realize
that stress and conflict can lead to violent behavior.
Young people should not be afraid to get help.

Peer Mediation

Peer mediation is a program that many schools have
developed to help students resolve conflicts. Such programs have been enormously successful in reducing
violence among teens.

In peer mediation programs, students are trained to
resolve disagreements between other students. They
learn how to get each party in a disagreement to present
their side of the story in a non-threatening manner. In
some schools the mediators may work in teams.

Some mediators use a technique called role playing.
In role playing, the parties in a disagreement are asked
to act out the conflict and to consider possible solutions
in the process. After several suggestions are made, both

sides agree to a plan to resolve their differences. When a solution is reached, both people sign a mediation agreement, which clearly explains how they have agreed to resolve their differences.

Change Your Way of Thinking

There is no absolute way to guarantee that you will not be affected by an act of violence committed by another teen. But there are things you can do to reduce the likelihood. The best way is to think—and act—in a positive way. Sound too simple? Could be, but if it were all that easy for everyone to do, there would be no need for this book.

Stay in school. In school you will learn skills for dealing with life. Avoid drugs and alcohol, which are a frequent catalyst for violence. If you are involved with gangs, get out. This can be difficult, but it is not impossible. Many schools offer a program called GREAT (Gang Resistance Education and Training), which was developed by police officers to steer teens away from gangs. Find positive activities that you enjoy—clubs, after-school groups, community organizations, sports, or volunteer programs.

If you have trouble with drugs, alcohol, or gangs, find an adult who will help you. Many schools offer SAP, or Student Assistance Programs. SAP counselors work with students to help them to stay in school, stay away from drugs and gangs, and look for solutions to their problems without turning to violence. SAP team members may include teachers, counselors, nurses, and social workers.

Many schools and communities offer mentoring programs. One of the first organizations to provide this service were the Big Brothers/Big Sisters of America. In a mentoring program, a student is assigned an adult who acts as both a friend and teacher. The mentor is someone to whom teens can turn when they need help. While many mentors spend time taking students on camping trips or to ball games, others help students with their homework or simply talk to them about the problems that teenagers face today.

Other programs are local. For example, the TAGS program (Teens Against Gangs) was developed in Springfield, Illinois. TAGS teaches teens to recognize gang signs or colors and to steer away from areas of potential trouble. A judge in Indiana started a program called not "Not in My Neighborhood," which sponsors workshops for parents and students. These include a videotape in which the viewer becomes a juror in a trial concerning a teen shooting that took place in a schoolyard. The discussions and debates that follow are designed to help young people think about their actions and the consequences of them.

Shoot Hoops, Not Guns

One nationwide community program that has met with much success is the "Midnight Basketball" program. The group was started in 1986 with the help of money

The Big Brothers/Big Sisters program provides mentoring to children and teens at risk.

from the federal government. It allows certain playgrounds and recreation centers to be staffed so that they can stay open well into the night, giving young people a safe place to play organized sports.

Cities such as Philadelphia have sponsored gun turn-in programs. Anyone who turns in a gun to the police receives a reward of either cash or gift certificates that can be used at local stores. The police promise not to ask any questions about where the guns came from. If you are concerned about the number of guns in your community, urge your parents to vote and express their support for gun-control legislation.

Perhaps your community has similar programs. If not, and you see a need for one, maybe you and your friends could work with concerned adults to start one. Individuals cannot completely solve the problem of teen violence, but they can help make a big difference. There are many places to get help and a lot of people willing to steer young people in the right direction.

Dameon was one of Michael Bennett's many friends. The two boys took karate lessons together. At Michael's funeral, Dameon was overcome by seeing the coffin that held his friend's body. "I get chills when I go in there," he said.

Matlyn did not know Michael Bennett. She was friends with one of the boys who attacked him. Still, she felt that she should go to Michael's funeral. "I feel kind of awkward," she said at the church, "like I don't

If your community does not have programs for young people, work with concerned adults to start one.

belong here. I guess I just had to make it real—that the boy is actually gone by the hand of someone I know. This could have been my brother, you know?"

Glossary

census Activity performed by the government
to count the number of people living in a
particular area.

counselor A person trained to give advice and help
other people.

grief The process of suffering a person undergoes
when a loved one dies.

homicide The killing of one human being
by another.

juvenile According to the laws of most states, a person younger than eighteen years of age.

mediation A process of working out a fair solution
to a problem or disagreement between two or
more people.

mentor An older friend or counselor who provides
help, advice, and support.

psychologist A person trained in the science of the
human mind and behavior.

sociologist A person trained in the study of society
and social relationships.

stress A feeling of strain or tension as the result of
various events in a person's life. Too much stress
can produce both physical and emotional symptoms.

vandalism The intentional damage or destruction of
property that belongs to others

Where to Go for Help

American Academy of Pediatrics
Division of Publications
141 Northwest Point Blvd.
P.O. Box 927
Elk Grove Village, IL 60009-0927

Bureau of Alcohol Tobacco and Firearms
(to report a crime involving gangs, drugs, or firearms)
(800) 283-4867

Center to Prevent Handgun Violence
1225 I Street NW
Washington, DC 20005

Children's Creative Response to Conflict (CCRC)
523 North Broadway
Nyack, NY 10960
(914) 358-4601
e-mail: fornatl@ign.apc.org

National Center for Injury Prevention and Control
Division of Violence Prevention
Mailstop K60
4770 Buford Highway
Atlanta, GA 30341-3724
(770) 488-4646

National Crime Prevention Council
(202) 466-6272

United States Department of Justice Kids' Page
Office of Juvenile Justice and Delinquency Prevention
Washington, DC 20531
Web site: http://www.usdoj.gov/kids.page/

For Further Reading

Bode, Janet. *Death Is Hard to Live With*. New York: Bantam, 1993.

Christensen, Loren. *Skinhead Street Gangs*. Boulder, CO: Paladin Press, 1994.

Ewing, Charles Patrick. *When Children Kill*. Lexington, MA: Lexington Books, 1990.

——— *Kids Who Kill*. Lexington, MA: Lexington Books, 1990.

Hamburg, Beatrix. *Violence in America's Classes*. New York: Cambridge University Press, 1998.

Kreiner, Anna. *Everything You Need to Know About School Violence*. New York: Rosen Publishing Group, 1996.

Nathan, Amy. *Everything You Need to Know About Conflict Resolution*. New York: Rosen Publishing Group, 1996.

Sickmund, Melissa, Howard N. Snyder, and Eileen Poe-Yamagata. *Juvenile Offenders and Victims: 1997 Update on Violence*. Washington, DC: Office of Juvenile Justice and Delinquency Prevention, 1997.

Stark, Evan. *Everything You Need to Know About Family Violence*. New York: Rosen Publishing Group, 1997.

Index

About the Author

Jeffrey A. Margolis is the author of several books on teens and violence. He is a guidance counselor at a junior high school in southern New Jersey.

Photo Credits

Cover photo & pp. 36, 40, 58 © Brian Silak; pp. 2, 26, 34, 56 © AP/ Wide World; p.8 © Reuters/ Pool /Archive Photos; p.24 © Corbis/Genevieve Naylor; p.24 © The Granger Collection; p.10 © Ira Fox; p.13 © Daniel Brody; p.15 © Sarah Friedman; p.21 © John Novejosky; p.30 © John Bentham; p.47 © Michael Brandt; p.52 © Pablo Maldonado.